MARY ENGELBREIT'S
HOME COMPANION

fabric

Projects & Creative Decorating Ideas

Text by Vitta Poplar

Photography by Barbara Elliott Martin

**Andrews McMeel
Publishing**

Kansas City

www.andrewsmcmeel.com
www.maryengelbreit.com

Library of Congress Cataloging-in-Publication Data
Poplar, Vitta.
   Fabric : projects and creative decorating ideas / text by Vitta Poplar; photography by Barbara Elliott Martin.
      p. cm.
   "Mary Engelbreit's home companion."
   Includes index.
   ISBN 0-7407-0999-2
   1. House furnishings. 2. Textile fabrics in interior decoration. I. Martin, Barbara Elliott. II. Title.

TT387 .P67 2001
747'.9--dc21

                                                                    00-046432

MARY ENGELBREIT'S HOME COMPANION
EDITOR IN CHIEF: Mary Engelbreit
EXECUTIVE EDITOR: Barbara Elliott Martin
ART DIRECTOR: Marcella Spanogle

First Edition
10 9 8 7 6 5 4 3 2 1

PRODUCED BY SMALLWOOD & STEWART, INC., NEW YORK CITY
DESIGNER: Alexis Siroc

PRINTED IN ITALY

ATTENTION: SCHOOLS AND BUSINESSES
Andrews McMeel books are available at quantity discounts with bulk purchase
for educational, business, or sales promotional use. For information, please write to:
Special Sales Department, Andrews McMeel Publishing, 4520 Main Street, Kansas City, Missouri 64111.

contents

introduction

In my first apartment, I used my mother's tablecloths as curtains out of economic necessity. Nowadays, I find myself doing similar things—but for different reasons. I'm still drawn to the one-of-a-kind look you get when you create your own designs, working with fabrics in ways they weren't originally intended to be used. I've turned dish-towel fabric into skirts on chair slipcovers, popcorn chenille bedspreads into shower curtains, embroidered tea cloths into valances. And the results have always been exactly as I envisioned, not something a decorator decided for me.

If you were to drop in to my studio, you'd see that despite the fact that I'm an illustrator, fabric is just as important to me as drawing tools. When I'm working, it's fun to have an interesting pattern to refer to, whether to draw wallpaper, the print on a little girl's dress, or the upholstery on a sofa. And many of the fabrics that I've simply invented in my drawings have actually come to life as real textiles.

It's funny that way: Using fabric is really just another way of painting, tossing color around, setting a mood, creating depth and shadows. Just throw a paisley shawl or a Navajo saddle blanket over a chair, and you've changed the chair. It's really that easy. So dig into your linen closet and see what you come up with— maybe you'll find a curtain that would look nice as a tablecloth?

Happy fabric hunting,

Mary Engelbreit

chapter

a world of styles

the magic of textile

Florals over lace over stripes?
If you love textiles, it all
coordinates, OPPOSITE. Even
one panel of pattern—an
African Kuba textile woven
of raffia—adds dimension
to a canvas-covered 1960s
chair, ABOVE, and makes it
the focal point of the room.

f all the do-it-yourself projects, decorating
with fabric is often perceived as the most
challenging, even though it is probably the most
rewarding. People willing to grab a chair at auction, plot
a garden, or try decorative paint finishes can freeze up
in front of a half-dozen swatches. The fact is, however,
that the principles that apply to choosing furniture,
planting flowers, and, yes, sponge-painting—color, line,
texture, placement—are similar for fabric. Since fabric
is lightweight and can usually be switched around on
a whim, trying out new ideas is a snap. If you let go
of preconceived notions and free your mind to imagine
the possibilities, you can decorate with fabric.

Durable cotton is the casual, washable fabric of choice for cushions, tablecloth, and curtains in a blue-themed kitchen, LEFT. A slipcover of sturdy floral canvas—a blend of linen, hemp, and cotton— makes a hammock, RIGHT, especially lush and inviting.

cultivate
the casual

For most of us, fragile fabrics in the living areas of our homes are just a fantasy. Those white silk curtains look good in a magazine, but in reality, wouldn't some rooms be better off with fabrics that can be tossed in the wash?

When buying fabric for everyday life, it pays to be a material person. You have to know what it is—and how it will wear—to make informed choices. For starters, fabrics come in three categories: naturals, such as cotton, linen, silk, and wool; synthetics, such as nylon or acrylic, which are often stronger, cheaper, more fade-resistant; and blends, which combine natural and synthetic fibers. Sometimes the blend is the ideal option, offering the traditional qualities of the natural *and* the durability of the synthetic.

When considering a fabric, examine the weave: a plain, tight weave with a high thread count per square inch tends to hold up best. Common sense dictates that if you can see through a fabric, it's not the best choice for covering a wing chair. But even if a material is heavy, it's not necessarily guaranteed to wear well. Look for a balanced weave in which the vertical and horizontal fibers are of the same weight and composition. The fabric's "hand," or the texture and quality of the surface, should be very even, with no ribs or raised fibers.

Before buying bolts upon bolts, subject fabrics to a "real life" test. Bring home about a half yard each of several contenders and experiment with them: scratch them with your nails, run a coin or a key over them, try pulling them apart, toss them in the wash. May the most durable (and adorable) fabric win.

plaids in check

While plaids are multiple stripes that cross at right angles, checks—close cousins to plaids—are a simple pattern of squares. Big, robust checks, OPPOSITE, infuse a tiny room with lively bungalow charm. The motif is echoed in the transom between the windows and the net hammock above the bed. A host of plaids LEFT, mixes easily to create a vibrant, informal atmosphere in a snug winter sitting room.

gingham to make you smile

Like a tall glass of lemonade
for your rooms, gingham
freshens the look. Draped
over a table and upholstered
on a footstool, LEFT, it
dresses a living room for
summer. For cottage charm,
scatter gingham pillows,
ABOVE, over the seat of a
simple wood settee. This plain
but cheerful woven cotton
is at home in any room and is
a friend to polka dots and
other winsome patterns.

ticking keeps

on going

Originally a covering for mattresses, linen or cotton ticking has a strength and simplicity that make it useful in many ways. A pinstriped mattress and an awning-striped pillow, OPPOSITE, offer comfort on a screened porch. Identified by tight, diagonal twill weaves and narrow stripes on a white or cream background, ticking comes in countless varieties; mixing them, ABOVE, will instantly conjure a summer-house mood. Big pieces of vintage ticking, LEFT, are available at tag sales and antiques shows.

A chenille throw hangs beside a deep-hued woolen blanket in a dining room corner, RIGHT. "I use both as tablecloths on outdoor furniture in the fall," says Linda, LEFT, with Stu. The floral drapes are new, "a formal touch that adds a bit of romance," she muses.

The Davidsons' camp aesthetic

fabric workshop

When Linda Davidson found a vintage bark-cloth fabric with "twelve drapery panels covered with standing grizzly bears, stags, and men carrying canoes," she was ecstatic. Typically, she would have sold the fabric through her home-based antiques business specializing in lodge and cabin-look collectibles; instead, she vowed to use it in the lakeside Georgia home she shares with her fisherman husband, Stu. When Linda isn't doing antiques shows, she's scouring the back roads of the Great Lakes region and the Adirondack Mountains of New York State. "I never have a problem finding wonderful textiles. There is no shortage, even though people have a greater appreciation of homespun fabrics than ever before," she says. "When you have a rustic home with lots of wood like I do, the textiles are essential for providing color and softening the look."

"Layering vintage fabrics is my best strategy for showing off lots at a time," says Linda. Stu's family quilts, which date from the 1920s, fold back to reveal a 1950s plaid spread, FAR LEFT. Featuring flying geese, a 1930s cotton-linen bark cloth—so called for its nubbly texture—is eye-catching as upholstery, ABOVE. Souvenir balsam pillows, LEFT, are from early-20th-century road trips.

Damask's elegance lies in its subtlety: The pattern plays across the ground in a single color. When you contrast a damask with a multicolor patterned fabric—as on a daybed canopy, RIGHT—the effect is heightened. Bullion fringe skirting the edge of a damask panel, LEFT, makes it all the more lavish.

living with luxury

Luxury is as comforting as a childhood blanket if the look is easy, as if the fabrics and furnishings have always been there. Think Tuscan villa in a hill town or Scottish castle on the moors. Even the names of luxury fabrics convey a regal charm. Brocade, whose raised patterns resemble embroidery, is an ideal heavy upholstery (though the raised fibers can catch). Damask, a mix of plain and lustrous weaves, has a formal air that suits draperies as well as it does slipcovers. Matelassé is another lush textile whose double weave gives it an embossed look; long used in elegant bedcovers, it now lends its luxe boudoir aura throughout the home. And taffeta: Crisp and plain, it retains its shape with little support, like a sweeping ballgown. Pair it with velvet, a cut pile that shimmers in candlelight, and your rooms will appear to have been lifted from an enchanted kingdom.

so worldly, silk

A length of silk swagged over the window and silk ties draped over the armoire, FAR LEFT, provide finishing touches both stately and casual in a gentleman's dressing room. On a smaller scale, the drape of a silk scarf, ABOVE, acts as a soft foil for a collection of metal objects. Because it absorbs dye so well, silk can be colored in a variety of rich jewel tones, LEFT.

stripes add texture

Walls painted an aqua stripe,
RIGHT, anchor a living room,
while striped silk taffeta
curtains that hold their jaunty
flared shape add depth. A
muted brocade daybed and
tapestry pillows, ABOVE, with
color and texture reminiscent
of an oil painting, are lovely on
their own. Toss in the striped
damask pillow that echoes
the gilt-framed oval portrait
on the wall and your eyes are
awakened by the contrast.

kids have a

zeal for chenille

In 1895, Catherine Evans Whitener of Dalton, Georgia, came up with a unique pattern for a bedspread, based on a French dressmaking technique called chenille. The design, which was a wedding gift for her sister, was so popular that it spawned an entire industry. For children's rooms, THESE PAGES, reproduction and recycled chenille bedspreads in ice cream parlor colors become wonderful upholstery on chairs and an ottoman, pillows, and even a translucent pinwheel window shade.

Curtains don't have to obscure your windows. Two tabbed gossamer panels entwined in strands of ivy, RIGHT, frame a pair of windows as if they were one. Long, barely-there curtains, LEFT, provide a sense of enclosure without blocking light in an artist's studio.

light-as-air translucents

The words whisper like petals on a breeze: dotted swiss, batiste, voile, plissé, piqué. These filmy, see-through fabrics appeal to our romantic side, irresistibly breezy in warm weather and a sun-welcoming gift in darker months of the year. Whether they're in curtains, valances, screens, or bed canopies, these dreamlike materials softly filter sunshine and lighten the mood of a room. The layered, translucent effect lends itself to such embellishments as beading, appliqué, and embroidery; yet sheers never overpower, so you can use them with abandon.

A wonderful range of sheer fabrics exists beyond the slippery polyester varieties that once seemed de rigueur behind living room curtains. Fabric stores offer organdy, chiffon, tulle, and muslin alongside more traditional translucents. And sheer doesn't always mean white: Look for watercolor-soft florals and stripes.

sheer pleasure

Without obscuring the bay of dramatic windows—or the flow of sunlight—in the bedroom of a Philadelphia house, LEFT, simple sheers form a subtle continuum with pale orange walls. Because filmy fabrics swag and drape so easily, they are also a natural for casual decorating schemes: Tossed decoratively over a four-poster bed, ABOVE, cascading sheers and branches of feathery white pine create a festive winter mood.

for the

love of lace

A lace panel suspended from a pole becomes a "head-board," OPPOSITE, while tiny white holiday lights behind the panel give the material a soft, warm glow. Lace curtains make great tablecloths, and conversely, an old lace table-cloth is perfect for lending privacy to a bathroom window without blocking light, LEFT. In another transformation, a large lace panel uncovered at a church bazaar, ABOVE, is framed under a sheet of glass and displayed like a painting above a living room mantel.

In a painter and printmaker's Arizona studio, LEFT, wild desert-colored patterns play backdrop for a cast of vivid paintings. A mid-century chair, RIGHT, is dressed for a party—noisemakers included—in a more traditionally striped serape of southwestern hues.

pattern making

Picture the luscious sight of shelf upon shelf of folded fabrics, each row providing a tantalizing glimpse of patterns. Taken together, this tapestry of styles always appeals, never clashes. So why is it that we have so much trouble combining two or more fabrics? Many furnishings manufacturers produce ready-made coordinates that take all the guesswork out of mixing and matching textiles, but it's much more fun—as well as more fulfilling—to do it yourself.

Here are some helpful guidelines for mixing patterns that are guaranteed to get results. To create your own pattern mix, begin with the print you plan to cast in the room's starring role. Now, with swatch in hand, find two other fabrics that are related to it in some way. The patterns should harmonize in color, mood, or texture without being clones of the principal fabric you've chosen.

The trick is to use fabrics in proportion. The primary print—let's say it's a floral—would go on the most dominant pieces of furniture and maybe even the curtains. The intermediate print—a stripe, perhaps—looks perfect on less prominent pieces, such as an ottoman, or as upholstery on the seat of a straight-backed chair. And the small-scale print— maybe a tiny check—is fun for throw pillows or a curtain border that accents the large print. Of course, there's always room for improvisation. You'll want to experiment a little, based on the scale of the room or the color of the walls and the carpet. Toss in an heirloom patchwork quilt or a vintage throw or two for variety, and you've created a custom mix.

fresh
as a bouquet

The blue tones in throw pillows made from old 1940s floral curtains and tablecloths, OPPOSITE, harmonize as accents for the pale-denim-colored sofa. In novelist Ciji Ware's California cottage, LEFT, matching cotton florals on the upholstered seating and scattered throw pillows create a burst of rosy color in an otherwise all-white room.

the story of toile

Toile de Jouy, a printed
pictorial fabric introduced in
France in the late 18th
century, lines a bed canopy,
LEFT, that teams up with
matching lampshades. Toile's
pleasures show off beautifully
across large upholstered
seating, walls, and flat drapery
panels but also work well in
an accent piece: Checks and
toiles are combined on a
single pillow, ABOVE, to create
a French country atmosphere.

three decades of prints

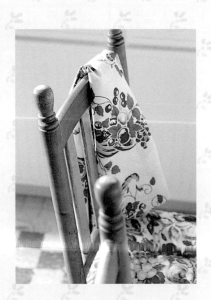

In the 1930s and 1940s, tablecloths with maps of Florida hit the souvenir shops of Miami Beach. An excellent specimen, RIGHT, complements other tablecloths from the same era that have been reinvented as valances. In the 1940s, linen cambric tea towels, ABOVE, were often given as wedding gifts. A perky floral cloth from the 1950s, LEFT, brings some retro sunshine into a kitchen.

discovering the past

"We took an old cherry-motif tablecloth and turned it into a lampshade," says Joan Stevens, a collector and sometime dealer in St. Louis, who supplied the fabric to outfit Mary Engelbreit's vintage kitchen. Joan guesses that the cherries cloth came from the late 1940s or early 1950s. "Dating a tablecloth is not an exact science, but you can often tell the era by matching it up with the colors and patterns of other kitchen things," she says. "Fiestaware often issued table-cloths in colors coordinated to the china." When a tablecloth is stained, Joan salvages the good parts for valances, shirt pockets, or pillows. Note the curtains, too, which are made from 1940s feed sacks.

how to make...
a printed-fabric lampshade

Designed by Mary Engelbreit

shopping list

- old wooden lamp base
- sandpaper
- paint and brush
- lampshade frame
- piece of vintage fabric
- large rickrack
- thin white cord
- sewing supplies

1 prepare the lamp base

Sand the lamp base; paint it to complement the fabric.

2 sew the shade cover

Measure the circumference of the shade frame at the bottom, then measure the height. Cut a square of fabric 1 ½" longer than the circumference and 6" longer than the height. Fold the bottom edge under by ¼", then by ¼" again; press. Pin the rickrack in place along the edge, overlapping slightly. Sew through both the rickrack and fabric. Fold the fabric in half, right sides facing, and sew a ½" side seam. Turn right side out.

3 make a casing for the ruffle

Turn the top edge under by 2". Make a casing: Sew a seam ¾" down from the top, then sew a parallel seam ½" below that. Cut a small slit through the inside of the casing and feed the cord all the way through (attach a safety pin to one end of the cord to guide it along its way); both ends of the cord should protrude.

4 finish the shade

Slip the cover over the frame. Pull the cord until the top fits; tie a bow and trim excess. Arrange the ruffle evenly.

2

expressions

personalizing the look

A cheerful design of wreaths and swags on curtain panels, ABOVE, brightens a rustic kitchen. Mixed with other vivid patterns in a dining room, OPPOSITE, **Middle Eastern kilim rugs—popular in the 1960s—make a comeback as side chair upholstery.**

For a moment, pretend that you know nothing about the "rules" of decorating with fabric. How and where can you splash it around the house? You might paper your walls with patterned fabric. One striped flat bedsheet, decorated with braided trim and punched with grommets, could become a shower curtain. Two floral flat sheets, stitched together, could be pressed into service as a duvet cover. While you're at it, try using vintage evening gowns from your grandmother's trunk as curtains or room dividers, suspended from crochet-covered hangers. Think of textiles as raw art materials and you'll never again pass a fabric shop without dropping in, if only for a peek.

Rather than mothballing extra fabric, reinvent it. Plaid balloon shades, LEFT, began life as flannel sheets. Try molding fabric into soft sculpture: Stacked-up tablecloths, RIGHT, become a patterned pedestal.

double your pleasure

Do you flunk tests that entreat you to find your true decorating style? Some of us have several styles—depending on our state of mind, the season, or our stage of life, so there's no reason to tie yourself to one look. Open up the possibilities: Whip up some fabric "sandwiches" that capture your different moods. For instance, create a coverlet that shows off a practical striped-wool haberdashery motif on one side and soft silk on the other. Make a throw of luxurious peony-pink velvet sewed back-to-back with a neutral sand-colored linen. Toss it over a chaise, velvet or linen side up, depending on how your day went. Or go all out and layer the fabrics one right over the other—maybe a softly faded chintz tablecloth over a longer skirt with a bold trellis pattern. Sometimes the fun is in showing off a material where you'd least expect it: Choose a 1950s conversation print with cowboys and lassos as the lining of an otherwise formal damask curtain, for example.

St. Louis interior designer Suzy Grote knows how fabrics are "supposed" to be used. She was once curator of the historic Fraunces Tavern in New York City, as well as a decorative arts expert with the Brooklyn Museum. Her advice: "There's something really boring and rigid about having only historically correct materials and playing by the rules. It's lots more fun to play with bold patterns. Trust your eye. It'll tell you when you've got it right." So if you find yourself torn between a teacup-printed fabric and one with a tropical-fruit theme, splurge on both. It's like being allowed to have two desserts.

quilts
off the bed

If you have more quilts than beds, don't lock them in the linen closet. Quilts hung on pegs, OPPOSITE, perform the same task as wallpaper—and they're easier to take down! Or display them folded over the rungs of a library ladder or suspended from a pole with Velcro strips. Damaged full-size quilts can easily be turned into throw pillows, LEFT, for a den.

the art of the pillow

Think of pillows as paintings for a sofa or daybed, FAR LEFT. Indulge your taste for luxury with them, since a little fabric goes a long way. Use an image-transfer kit or have a professional service actually transfer photos onto fabric, ABOVE. While you're at it, further personalize pillows, LEFT, with buttons, lace, and some favorite trimmings from the sewing box.

that French "certain something"

Just for a moment, consider where the vintage French indienne cotton fabric that now covers these pillows may have been. Perhaps it was once a tablecloth in a Provençal cottage. Or an upholstery fabric on a sun-flooded terrace in Paris's Third Arrondissement. For Barbara Ashford, part owner of Henhouse, an antiques emporium in Birmingham, Alabama, both the romance of vintage fabrics and their time-mellowed warmth are reason enough to feature them on an iron daybed in her guest cottage. (The quilt is another French antique.) Small amounts of secondhand textiles lend themselves to little projects like pillows and chair cushions; if you still don't have enough to go around, add a border of a complementary contemporary fabric.

how to sew...
a fringed fabric
pillow sham

A design from Henhouse

shopping list

- 1 yard floral fabric 54" wide
- ½ yard plaid fabric
- 3 yards fringe
- 24" square pillow insert
- sewing supplies

1 assemble the front

Cut one square of floral fabric 19" x 19". Cut four pieces of plaid fabric 25" x 4". With the right sides facing, and leaving a ½" seam allowance, sew the long edges of the plaid strips to the main piece. Miter each corner, trim the miter seams to ½", and press flat.

2 prepare the back

Cut two pieces of floral fabric 25" x 16". Hem one long edge of each piece: Fold the fabric in by ¼", then again by ½", press, and sew along the folded edge. With right sides facing, lay the pillow back pieces over the pillow front, lining up the outer edges so the hemmed edges of the back pieces overlap each other.

3 complete the sham

Insert the fringe (with the cut end facing inward) between the two pillow layers, all the way around. Pin in place, easing the fringe at the corners. Sew ½" in from the edge all the way around. Go around a second time to reinforce the stitches. Turn the pillow sham right side out and insert the pillow.

A quilted wall hanging, RIGHT, shows how black makes even subdued colors pop. Chicago textile artist Jane Sassaman plots her creations on paper before cutting cloth. She seeks out "weird" shades like lime green and a rosy fuchsia, LEFT.

color boldness

There's actually a science to choosing can't-miss color combinations: Just stick to the color wheel. Analogous colors are close together on the disk, while complementary colors are opposite one another. What's perhaps most satisfying about experimenting with the color wheel is personalizing a palette: using radiant jewel box shades (magenta, Prussian blue, viridian) or vowing to decorate only in one color (claret, burgundy, cerise) down to the last dinner napkin. While few color consultants would advocate a bubblegum-pink pillow on an aqua bedspread or coral drapes with milk-chocolate chairs, most would admit that often it's best just to follow your instincts. Cloth and paint from the past have faded, but scientists are certain that our forebears lived on veritable pigment overload, surrounded by imperial yellow, pea green, and ripe pumpkin. Isn't it time for a revival?

a call for color

A bedroom, LEFT, looks like a color convention, but check closely and you'll see that the knotty-pine walls are fairly subdued. It's the bedspreads, adorned with patches of saturated color and rickrack borders, that provide the spark. Red, yellow, and blue add extra zing to a valance on a kitchen door, ABOVE; an odd selection of hats repeats the cheerful color scheme.

Though Swedish-made, this sofa throw in a second-floor hall, RIGHT, has the verve of bold West African colors. Not all of the continent's colors are the same: "North Africa is known for pastels," says Sharne Algotsson, LEFT.

Sharne Algotsson's bold palette
fabric workshop

Sharne Algotsson is taken with Africa. "The crafts-people are college educated. They want to go back to their traditional art forms. And they're reinterpreting old motifs in wonderful new ways, like silk screening." Studying the nuances of African design has driven the Philadelphia designer and author for two decades, starting when she was a graduate student traveling in Ghana. A few years later, when she married and moved to Sweden, she discovered more weavers. "I became aware of the large-scale geometric prints from Marimekko and designers like Josef Frank," she says. Today, Sharne uses African textiles for trim on Eurostyle window treatments and tablecloths, as pillows, and even as duvets. But you needn't travel to Africa to find material, Sharne points out. "Most any large city has specialty stores that carry wonderful cloths."

"Rough and refined combined" is how Sharne describes her style. Orange is her choice for raw-silk Austrian shades in the dining room, FAR LEFT, and burlap-weight linen curtains in the kitchen, ABOVE. The cloth on a table just big enough for coffee and the morning paper is a strip-woven cotton blanket from Mali. A tone-on-tone diamond-patterned sofa, LEFT, represents the household's European side.

fantastic contrasts

If your rooms are slumbering, awaken them with accents! In a Florida living room, RIGHT, eyes are drawn directly to the seating and the graphic pillows made from Guatemalan fabric. A monochromatic interior, ABOVE, perks up with a crimson Gumby-shaped chair and rhinoceros pillow. A decorating scheme based on the extremes of black and white, LEFT, exploits the attraction of opposites.

To expand a white room even more, use pools of cucumber-cool shades like sea foam and aqua. In a beach house, LEFT, pillows add subtle waves of faded color. Light-gray muslin shirts, RIGHT, provide gentle contrast in an all-white decor.

white delight

Even if you've never studied the Chinese art of design called feng shui, you're a practitioner if you decorate with white. In a universe ranging from eggshell and arctic ice to vanilla ice cream and beige, the tenets couldn't be more specific: Use warm whites (those with undertones of pink or yellow) in a bedroom or living room, where they'll create a cozy nest. Cooler shades (laced with blue, green, or purple) impart a feeling of order in baths and kitchens. For maximum interest, combine several fabrics: Display a log-cabin quilt in different shades of neutrals with scraps of twill, poplin, or nubby chenille. Swathe furniture in white canvas duck and cotton brocade slipcovers. Embellish wheat-toned cotton pillowcases with an edge of ivory silk. White frees the mind. You'll never tire of it—why else would the universe give us snow, surf, and lily of the valley?

accents on white

For a collection of toy-bright folk art in an Atlanta home, RIGHT, white makes an ideal neutral backdrop for viewing individual objects. Without its red flourishes, a creamy high-ceilinged room, ABOVE, would seem too vast and undefined for comfort. But sailcloth pillows with checked ruffle accents provide a grounding effect, as does the cardinal-stripe quilt at the footboard.

sounding the tones

By combining different tonal versions of a single hue, you'll create interiors that are naturally pleasing to the eye. In a Seattle, Washington, bungalow, LEFT, green—the color of vitality—turns to khaki, moss, and fir on a sofa. Textured fabrics introduce a hint of pattern without departing from the tone poem. A waffle-weave cotton throw, ABOVE, complements the serenity of plain jute flooring.

inspirations

channeling the muse

For the dedicated fabric collector, the day may come when you need a chart to remember what textiles you own. In fact, some collectors keep books of swatches on hand, complete with detailed notes on cloth type, yardage, date of purchase, and collectible value, if any, to jog their memories. Rather than just storing your fabric, we have another idea: Use it. Even a small amount can make a difference, perhaps as a "slipcover" for exposed wiring on a hanging lamp or staple-gunned to the frame of a folding screen, the edges masked by ribbon. If your material is truly rare, frame it with conservation-quality materials like acid-free backing and glass with UV protection.

Pillows can be small works of art, the fastenings design elements in themselves, like these bright buttons and ribbon ties, OPPOSITE. Knitted flag replicas, ABOVE, once a popular craft, become outsize club-chair pillows, "framed" by sky blue chambray panels.

Draped over a bed made of old posts and balusters, LEFT, a piece of crocheted lace suggests a lavishly feminine canopy. Scallop-skirted slip-covers in mix-and-match fabrics, RIGHT, bring a touch of lightheartedness to a set of formal dining chairs.

fabric first

f you've ever studied art, you know that fabric often plays a supporting role in paintings. Just think of the rich green dress in van Eyck's *The Arnolfini Marriage*, the brilliant red blanket in van Gogh's *Bedroom at Arles*, or the lush bed hangings in Courbet's *Venus and Psyche*. Of course, many other celebrated paintings include depictions of textiles that convey mood and meaning. Why not apply those ideas to your own rooms, letting fabric take the lead? Instead of attaching a headboard to your bed, suspend a vintage quilt, a silk sari, or a tapestry from a rod on the wall. Transform a bathtub with a gauzy canopy hung from plant hooks. Fabric can even stand in for paintings. Collectors of Marimekko prints from the 1970s display mounted squares of them on walls. Do your own take with textiles glued onto wood disks and hung like a free-floating Twister mat.

playing with layering

Texas textile whiz Janet Proch created a lavish dust ruffle, RIGHT, from linen gathered in pencil-point pleats. If you're not a seamstress, make one from old tablecloths stitched together and tucked between the mattress and the box spring. A late-Victorian yo-yo quilt, ABOVE, gives a dressing room corner an upholstered jewel box appearance.

slipcover madness

With slipcovers, you get to play Pygmalion to your furniture, truly transforming its character. Update tired pieces with a clean, contemporary look, like these pared-down neutral covers, FAR LEFT. The back of a slipcover is as important as the front—sometimes more so. Atlanta artist Martha Young adds interest with such dressmaker details as corset bows, ABOVE, and a heart sachet with a dangling tassel, LEFT.

turning new into old

Call it what you will—patchwork, grab-bag, or raggle-taggle
decorating—but combinations of fabrics can be more
beautiful than a single choice. Janet Proch, a "designer
gone mom" in Fredericksburg, Texas, gives the example of
a child-size slipcover whose small scale makes it a fast and
fun project. "I wanted to use old fabrics in these slipcovers,
but since they're for my kids, they also had to withstand
peanut-butter fingers and lots of washings," Janet says.
"So I took new ticking and florals from my sister's store,
Homestead, and fudged the patina by aging them with RIT
tan dye." The only vintage elements are the lacy table linens
sewed over the tops of the chairs, out of harm's way.

how to sew...
a chair slipcover
with a pocket

Designed by Janet Proch

- three different upholstery-weight fabrics (main piece, sides, and pocket); measure your chair to determine the amounts

- decorative lace or a tea towel with embroidered edges to use as trim

- sewing supplies

1 create the main piece

Measure and cut the main piece of fabric so that it covers the entire chair from front to back, plus 2" all around for seams. With the fabric on the chair, position the embroidered trim or lace across the top of the chair back, pin in place, and sew to the main piece. Depending on the trim you use, you may want to hem the fabric's raw edges before attaching it to the main piece.

2 add the side pieces

Measure and cut two side pieces, adding 1" all around for seams. With wrong sides facing out, pin sides to main piece. Leaving a ½" seam allowance, sew sides to main piece. Hem the bottom: Fold under by ¼", then again by ½", sewing close to the folded edge. Turn right side out.

3 add the pocket

Cut a rectangle of the third fabric for a pocket (about 3" smaller than width of the chair). Cut a piece of lace or embroidery to trim top edge. Pin together, with the trim facing wrong side of fabric. Sew a seam, then turn trim back toward the front. Turn the sides and bottom of the pocket under ½" and pin the pocket in place on the slip-cover. Sew around three sides close to the turned edge. Sew a parallel seam ⅛" away from the first to reinforce.

out of sight

With the curtains closed, you'd never know that there's a cozy spot just off the breakfast nook, OPPOSITE, in a Pacific Northwest home. Though small, the hideaway boasts a twin mattress, a phone, and bookshelves. Try making your own in an unused closet or a windowed alcove. In Mary Engelbreit's home office, ABOVE, a tension rod under a desk holds a gingham check curtain that whisks shut to disguise office supplies. Fabric purses holding games pieces, LEFT, look like giant tassels hanging from a table.

Picnic-check place mats, LEFT, become tie-on cushions in a breakfast nook. Self-adhesive hook-and-loop fastening tape is a no-sew alternative. In the eye of the imaginative seamstress, even feed sacks, RIGHT, can be reincarnated as pillows or kitchen curtains.

transformations

Y ou're in luck. The weather forecaster just predicted downpours all weekend. Now is the time to tackle those rainy-day projects you've been meaning to do. So unpack all of your craft materials, keep a few takeout menus handy, and give fabrics the run of the house.

Think of sprinkling textiles around the way a thoughtful host puts out bowls of candy and fruit. You could take a favorite find—a madras panel from that trip to Nepal, for example—and roll it taffy style around an old bolster, cinching the ends with ribbons. Or fill a wicker picnic basket with a delicious feast of odds and ends—vintage bark cloth, quilt scraps, a monogrammed hankie— and put it on a coffee table for guests to dip into at will. For your home office, make a memory board from an old or a new picture frame and cork panel cut to fit, lined in a raw-silk plaid. For the bath, line a panel from an old flour sack with white terry cloth and use it as a hand towel. Make an ironing-board cover from your mother's Hawaiian luau dress from the 1950s.

Or let cloth turn design flaws into assets. If you live in a city loft, for instance, you could tie-dye muslin, then loop and swag it around exposed pipes. Disguise cracked walls by painting plain cotton duck with acrylics (mix in wallpaper paste for texture) and hanging it from quilt rods. Fabric also allows you to reproportion awkward spaces: Fashion an Indian-bazaar canopy that billows on trapeze-style ceiling rods and trails down the walls, hiding peculiar angles.

doing
double duty

Doorways, OPPOSITE, offer two different opportunities to use fabric imaginatively. The closet door beneath a stair-case was entirely removed and the opening draped in fabric; a simple lace valance on the entry door's window has a softening effect. Tablecloths are great choices, and any leftovers can be recycled—just look at this adorable child's romper made from a damaged piece and finished off with checkerboard trim.

new beginnings

St. Louis artist Joy Christensen sewed vintage handkerchiefs together to create a bed canopy, LEFT; the spread is quilt batting sandwiched between hand-kerchiefs and a sheet. Antique French draperies were turned into bedspreads and shams, ABOVE. Vintage playsuits and nightgowns, RIGHT, are "wallpaper" in a guest room.

just for fun

Sometimes all it takes is a tiny flourish to change a look, like knotting a kerchief, OPPOSITE, around a bedpost. If you can embroider—or if your sewing machine can—address someone's attention to a simple envelope pillow, ABOVE. Here's a way to enjoy your favorite fabric without depleting the supply: Mount color photocopies of it on lightweight cardboard and fold into perky pinwheels, LEFT. You could also use the copies to decoupage lamp-shades or tabletops to pair with the original fabric.

Nature Lover, RIGHT, a work of textile art that measures 30 x 32 inches, grew out of the love Chris Roberts-Antieau, LEFT, feels for the forest near her home. The figure's dress is made of printed silk; the stars are stitched by hand.

Chris Roberts-Antieau: in stitches

fabric workshop

Her work is not so much about the fabric itself, says textile appliqué artist Chris Roberts-Antieau, as about how it's manipulated: "It's about cutting it, showing color against color, and stitching techniques. I try to make my work childlike, direct." Of course, finding the right fabrics is essential, and Chris keeps 18 feet of it stacked by color in her Ann Arbor, Michigan, studio. "I mostly work with ordinary cottons and flannels, though occasionally I'll find something unusual at a thrift store, like an apron, a satiny coat lining, or a great old shirt," she says. Using textured black cotton and a heavy fusible interfacing, Chris creates sturdy canvases. To these, she fuses her decorative fabrics, then stitches the details by hand or with a sewing machine. "The fun and interesting part," she says, "is making people think they're paintings from a distance."

Chris schedules appointments with her doodle pad, FAR LEFT, two or three times a month. "I go back and forth between serene, spiritually based drawings and completely funny pieces," she says. Examples of the extremes: Hand-dyed floating-clouds fabric, ABOVE, in Contemplating the Universe (36 x 38 inches) and Alpo, LEFT (16 x 26 inches), a work that pays tribute to her bulldog, a finicky eater.

Think beyond the expected rod and curtain. Thread spools, RIGHT, allow panels to swag atop each window; boat cleats or crystal doorknobs would work, too. An embroidered tablecloth folded over a tension rod, LEFT, makes a valance in Mary Engelbreit's guest room.

curtain calls

What do Elvis Presley and curtains have in common? Both became a major American preoccupation at around the same time. When the King reigned, broad picture windows and sliding glass patio doors had begun to replace the fireplace as a room's focal point, and curtains became essential to decorating. Today, Elvis no longer shocks, and curtains don't always come from the drapery department. Instead, they're more likely to spring from your imagination: Hold blue and white tab panels in place with faceted paperweight buttons; add a fringe of faux cherries to the edges. Attach tab tops with children's overall clasps. Tie back everyday muslin with cotton sneaker shoelaces for a casual look. Or dress up your curtains by scattering Velcro tabs on them and attaching fabric leaves, coffee cups, peace signs, moons—whatever seems fresh and funky.

windows

on whimsy

These ties, OPPOSITE, were embellished with tiny terra-cotta flowerpots. Other good choices are chandelier prisms and tassels. Textile paint can weave plain curtains into a room's color scheme; a freehand squiggle of sunshine yellow combines with a bee stencil, ABOVE. Birch-twig wreath tiebacks, LEFT, add sculptural texture to the window. So would garlands of silk flowers and faux greenery.

window dressing

Proving once and for all that even if a fabric isn't meant for curtains it can still stand in nicely, Atlanta designer Wendy Middleton found this stylish—and inexpensive—solution to trimming a kitchen window in a tiny apartment. Contemporary Italian cotton tea towels become valances with the simple addition of grommets and cording. You can also use tea towels in plaids or French jacquard. Or adapt a lace tablecloth as a graceful curtain panel with café clips. In other rooms of the house, hand-embroidered table runners and dresser scarves are perfect for entryway sidelights. Old-fashioned antimacassars make pretty valances, too, and often come equipped with their own tassels.

how to make...
a kitchen towel
Designed by Wendy Middleton
valance

shopping list

- three or four kitchen towels (we used waffle-weave cotton)
- metal grommets (and grommet tool)
- white cotton cord
- curtain rod and brackets
- sewing supplies

1 measure the window

You want this valance to gather softly, so use as many kitchen towels as will fill the width of the window when they are placed end to end, plus one extra towel.

2 sew the towels together

Align the stripes of two towels along the short sides. Overlap the existing hems by ½" and pin. Stitch towels together along each existing hem. Repeat with remaining towels until all the towels are sewed together.

3 add the grommets

Fold the top 1" edge of the valance toward the back, pin, and hem. Evenly space the grommets approximately every 6" along this doubled edge and attach, following the instructions for your grommet tool.

4 tie it up!

Cut a piece of cord 10" long for each grommet. Pull each length of cord through a grommet and, leaving a 1" loop, tie a double knot. Bring the knot toward the front of the grommet, trim the cord ends so they are even, and fray them slightly to create small tassels. Slide the curtain rod through the loops and hang the curtain.

With quick rollover hems, vintage bark cloth turns into table napkins, LEFT. The runner and chair caddies are made from ticking. For your next alfresco dinner party, wrap burlap around cutlery, RIGHT. Tuck in a flower or two and cinch with raffia.

finishing touches

So you've outfitted your home to perfection, but have you looked out the window? Think of Far Eastern pavilions where embroidered fabrics billow in archways and of English tea gardens full of chintz-covered tables, and you'll realize that the possibilities for outdoor decorating are whatever you make them. But let's start closer to home: You could re-create the fun outdoor settings of the 1950s by sewing or gluing a rickrack border on a plain canvas market umbrella and adding ball fringe or tassels. Perhaps you've admired a sheet printed with a vintage design—buy the king-size flat and treat it as a tablecloth. You could even use photo-transfer paper to add printed images to your canvas patio chairs and glider pillows. Old postcards showing scenes of Miami Beach hotels or the Atlantic City boardwalk are apropos. Next stop: slipcovers for your car! Just kidding.

outdoor endings

Have you ever noticed how fabric from warm climates tends to be bright? It has to be, to stand up to the brilliant sunshine. A Provençal-style tablecloth, RIGHT, creates a Mediterranean look on a St. Louis patio. A patriotic scene—without Fourth of July colors—is suggested by a not-quite-accurate flag, ABOVE, sewed from fabric scraps on plain white canvas.

resources

new textiles

Baranzelli
New York, NY
(212) 753-6511
www.baranzelli.com

The Curtain Exchange
New Orleans, LA
(504) 897-2444
*custom-made window treatments
and bedding on consignment*

Great American Quilt Factory
(800) 474-2665

Homestead
Fredericksburg, TX
(830) 990-5103

Schumacher
(800) 332-3384
call for local availability

Traditions by Pamela Kline
Claverack, NY
(518) 851-3975
www.traditionspamelakline.com
*retro-inspired fabrics such as
toile, tickings, and storybook
and document prints*

Waverly
(800) 423-5881
www.waverly.com
call for local availability

vintage textiles and textile restoration

**Linda Davidson
American Antiques**
Berkeley Lake, GA
(770) 448-2773
*camp-related textiles, blankets,
and bark cloth*

Michele Fox
Palisades, NY
(914) 359-1960
antique ticking

Gentle Arts
New Orleans, LA
(504) 895-5628
www.gentlearts.com
textile restoration

Sewtique
Groton, CT
(860) 445-7320
textile preservation and restoration

**Joan Stevens
American Doodah**
St. Louis, MO
(314) 962-6268
*feed and flour sacks, tablecloths, and
a wide variety of household cloths*

**Ruth Touhill
Stoneledge Antiques**
Dutzow, MO
(636) 458-3516
*vintage quilts, tea towels,
camp blankets*

textile artists and designers

Joni Ulman Lewis
(540) 372-7537
photo transfer artist

Chris Roberts-Antieau
Manchester, MI
(734) 428-3860

Ron Ronan
(413) 644-9994
photo transfer artist

Susan Sargent Designs
(800) 325-3466
upholstery, bedding, accessories

services

**Sharne Algotsson
Inside Design Ltd.**
Philadelphia, PA
(215) 224-7808
www.insidedesignltd.com

photoTextiles
(800) 388-3961
photo transfer service

A Personal Touch
(800) 203-3619, ext. 2848
photo transfer service

organizations

**The National Quilting
Association**
Ellicott City, MD
(410) 461-5733
www.NQAQuilts.org

**National Upholsterer's
Association, Inc.**
St. Paul, MN
(651) 523-0666
www.upholsteryjournal.com

mary engelbreit stores

Atlanta
North Point Mall
1212 North Point Circle
Alpharetta, GA 30022
(770) 667-0414

Brea
Brea Mall
1020 Brea Mall
Brea, CA 92821
(714) 255-0674

Chicago
Woodfield Shopping Center
N-130 Woodfield Mall
Schaumburg, IL 60173
(847) 240-1444

Dallas
Dallas Galleria
13350 Dallas Parkway, #2820
Dallas, TX 75240
(972) 716-0644

Denver
Cherry Creek Mall
#259 3000 East 1st Avenue
Denver, CO 80206
(303) 331-8052

Frisco
Stonebriar Centre
2601 Preston Road, #1026
Frisco, TX 75034
(469) 633-1759

Minneapolis
Mall of America
(1st floor, between
Nordstrom & Macy's)
160 West Market Street
Bloomington, MN 55425
(612) 854-8860

Nashville
Opry Mills
461 Mills Drive, #461
Nashville, TN 37214
(615) 514-6279

Newport Beach
Fashion Island
271 Newport Center Drive
Newport Beach, CA 92660
(949) 644-9313

St. Louis
Saint Louis Galleria
1142 Saint Louis Galleria
St. Louis, MO 63117
(314) 863-5522

Seattle
Bellevue Square
2086 Bellevue Square
Bellevue, WA 98004
(425) 451-9621

Washington, DC
Tysons Corner Center 7
978L Tysons Corner Center
McLean, VA 22102
(703) 734-6279

credits

So many wonderful, creative people have brought us into their homes to inspire you and me. I would like to thank them all from the bottom of my heart. Mary

PHOTOGRAPHY ON PAGES 8, 42 (BOTTOM), 58, 60-63, 64 (BOTTOM), 71, AND 87 BY GORDON BEALL; PAGE 66 BY CATHERINE BOGERT; PAGES 13, 14, 98 (TOP), 100, AND 101 BY CHERYL DALTON; PAGES 70 AND 83 BY MIKE JENSEN; PAGES 37, 55, 102, AND 104 BY ERIC JOHNSON; PAGES 9, 35, 41, 54, 64, 76, AND 89 (BOTTOM) BY JENIFER JORDAN; PAGE 28 (BOTTOM) BY MARK LOHMAN; PAGES 27 AND 52 BY BOB MAUER; PAGE 36 BY MATTHEW MILLMAN; PAGES 31, 48, 74, AND 98 BY BRAD SIMMONS; PAGES 28 (TOP) AND 29 BY JUDITH WATTS; PAGE 18 (TOP) BY HUGH WILKERSON AND ROWANN SANDERS. ALL OTHER PHOTOGRAPHY BY BARBARA ELLIOTT MARTIN.

index